Then *&* **Now**

TOTTON AND ELING

Welcome Home! VE Day, 8 May 1945, and Eling man Douglas Hobby is greeted warmly by residents of Downs Park Crescent after five years away from home, and four-and-a-half years in a prisoner-of-war camp. This scene was captured at the welcome home party for Trooper D. Hobby on his return home after spending over four years in Stalag 13a, Stamlager 13, in Austria. Douglas arrived home as the VE Day celebrations were in full swing and this photo shows the people of Downs Park making a presentation to him, through one of its youngest residents. In the background the top of the local blast shelter can be seen. Most people had shelters in their gardens then and blast shelters were for those caught outside during a sudden raid. The large carriage-built pram of 1940s fashion on view, and the event itself, makes this a moving record of an historic moment in time.

Then & Now
TOTTON AND ELING

Barbara Deacon, Terry Henry,
Michael Southgate, Cecil Dench and Sylvia Dench
for Totton and Eling Historical Society

TEMPUS

The railway signal box by the level crossing gates in Junction Road. James Harvey, seen here with his wife and granddaughter, between 1870 and 1880. Mr Harvey was chief porter at Totton station until his retirement in April 1890. He died on 16 January 1903. The Harvey family lived in the cottage here until it was converted into a signal box. A terrace of railway cottages was built nearby to house railway workers, now also demolished and replaced with maisonettes. The hand-operated gates could scarcely be seen during the thick fogs so common until the late 1950s, and vehicles were often heard banging into them. For many years the signal box stood as a sentinel in Junction Road, warning all that lengthy delays were possible. The building was a local landmark and many were sad to see it go, firstly to unmanned operation and then disappearing altogether when demolished in 1982. No such regrets would be expressed about the train gates, however, where the traffic queues are a long–standing problem.

First published 2003

Tempus Publishing Limited
The Mill, Brimscombe Port,
Stroud, Gloucestershire, GL5 2QG

British Library Cataloguing in Publication Data.
A catalogue record for this book is available from the British Library.

ISBN 0 7524 2985 X

Typesetting and origination by Tempus Publishing Limited
Printed in Great Britain by Midway Colour Print, Wiltshire

CONTENTS

Introduction

At the end of the last Ice Age, perhaps more than 6,000 years ago, the sea level rose over what is now southern England. The area of land now known as Southampton Water flooded. Into it the river known as the Test drained, providing a natural barrier between the peninsula of Southampton and the area of the New Forest.

Evidence of early man has been found locally. Nomadic Stone Age hunters left their weapons and flint tools, including arrowheads to be found. The Celtic peoples left their mark on the local landscape. Tatchbury Mount, noted by the great nineteenth-century fieldworker Heywood Sumner, appears to have been used as a fortified camp of some kind although there has been little excavation at the site. It is tempting to think that Tatchbury was one of the Celtic hill forts reduced by the Roman General Vespasian as he marched west to attack Maiden Castle in Dorset. A Celtic rapier has also been found at Testwood Lakes. The Romans left little evidence of their occupation here, though a Roman road is thought to have run along the Waterside through Totton to Nursling, perhaps to transport local New Forest pottery. The road may have passed Eling church as a coin of the mid-fourth century was found outside the church in the process of digging a septic tank.

The Saxons also left little material evidence of their occupation. The main evidence is in the very earliest place names for the area. Edlinges is of Saxon origin and Totton comes from 'Tota', the home of Tota's people. The Domesday Book noted that the area had a church, fishery, two mills and saltpans, as well as grazing for animals, particularly pigs. Eling was a large manor and belonged to the Saxon Crown, which indicates its importance. For much of the Middle Ages, Totton and Eling remained agricultural communities dominated by the church and the land. It suffered with the rest of the country disasters such as the Black Death, and rejoiced in the successes of the Hundred Years War against the French. This pattern would continue throughout the period of the Tudors and Stuarts. The church was re-ordered on the demand of Cromwell's commissioners during the sixteenth-century Reformation, and Royalists and Cavaliers clashed at Redbridge.

It was not until the late eighteenth and nineteenth centuries that great change started to occur. Shipbuilding was given a boost by the Napoleonic Wars, with several large ships being built at Eling. Also in the mid-nineteenth century, Eling was developed as a port, stimulated by the construction of the railway from Southampton to Dorchester. By 1850 Totton had a railway station and a spur line ran to Eling quay. Slowly the area became more industrial than agricultural. The population began to grow and lines of red-brick housing appeared in Eling. Also a more subtle change took place – after the mid-nineteenth century, Totton became the dominant partner in relation to Eling, and housing development started to concentrate in the north of Totton.

In the twentieth century the growth of Totton and Eling accelerated. New building in the west and the north increased the population to nearly 30,000. A new shopping precinct has been built and much of the old character of the village has disappeared. Totton is now a town – not, as it once was – the largest village in England.

In many ways the troubles affecting Totton in the late nineteenth and early twentieth centuries seem to be summed up by the division of the community; first by the railway in the nineteenth century and then the bypass in the twentieth century. Built during the 1930s when traffic was much less prevalent, the bypass is more notorious to travellers than the train gates. It became such a local feature that, until recent times, a local parish magazine was called *The Flyover!* Rush hours are perhaps wrongly named on the bypass, as the traffic does anything but rush.

Totton's transition from a village to a town has not been easy. Until very recently its traffic pattern and congestion had been determined by decisions taken when Totton was a village. In recent times plans have come and gone; a new road was cut from Ringwood Road roundabout to Junction Road to take traffic from Totton's congested centre, but it terminates at the train gates. The more recent Totton western bypass takes some traffic away but, typical of the district, is not wide enough in places to take four lanes of traffic. A recent town centre plan has suggested more major changes but the basic problems still remain – how to reduce the queues at the train gates and how to ease the traffic congestion on the roads through the town.

It was during this period of change, especially in the late twentieth century, that the Totton and Eling Historical Society formed. Its members consist of residents and people no longer living in the district. Many of its early members come from the older parts of Eling. This is the area that still retains part of the old village atmosphere and remains an entity separated from Totton by the bypass. At first the society met to aid the restoration of Eling Tide Mill and to promote the creation of a local museum. It now has an extensive collection of old photographs, some of which appear in this publication, and also has monthly meetings at which topics of interest are discussed. The society also played a part with the local Town Council in setting up the Totton and Eling Heritage Centre, which has proved to be a popular local attraction along with the nearby world-famous Tide Mill.

The Heritage Centre was set up to reflect the development of Totton and Eling. The artefacts offered as gifts or on loan are varied, reflecting the changing aspects of life in the area – hence collections of material on both work and education, among other subjects that have been gathered. The society also obtained the birth, marriage, baptism and burial records for Eling Parish, which are now obtainable on microfiche. A collection of early prints illustrate the rural nature of village life, which today may seem hard to believe. The society holds exhibitions of local life and recently held 1940s and '50s exhibitions which proved very popular. Schools are encouraged to visit the centre and members of the society have visited local schools to share their memories with the children.

The society has produced a number of publications, such as the *It Happened to Us* booklet with its reminiscences of wartime, and another of memories of work at the British Power Boat Company written by former employees, many of whom lived locally. This proved especially popular. Several society members are currently undertaking research: most of the local school log books have been edited and work is continuing on the great country houses that existed in the area. The Historical Society continues to move ahead, tracking the past of the district before it is lost to memory.

The society may be contacted at: Eling Tide Mill, Eling Lane, Totton, SO40 9HF
or via the website: www.argonot.co.uk/users/eling.tidemill

By Terry Henry on behalf of Totton and Eling Historical Society

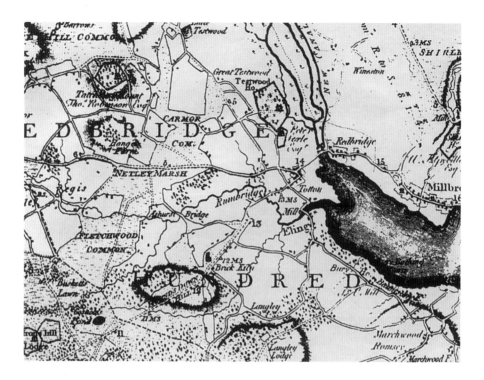

The district of Totton and Eling at the end of the eighteenth century. Detail from Milne's map of Hampshire, 1791. This illustrates how sparsely-populated the area was at that time, before the period of rapid growth which began in the Victorian era.

ACKNOWLEDGMENTS

Most of the illustrations in this book come from the Totton & Eling Historical Society's archives, collected over many years for the benefit of local residents. We would like to thank those people, too numerous to mention, who have entrusted us with their photographs during this time. We would especially like to thank the following for their contributions to this book: Pauline and William Abraham, Peter Avery, Derek Biggs, Sally Bishop, D. Blackwell-Eaton, Richard Brown, Rose Burt, Eling Sailing Club, Eling School, Jenny Keehan, Joyce Kemish, Marcus of Lymington, Dave Maton, Brian A. Moody, Ian Nelson, Planet News Ltd, A. Purrington, Totton Timber, James Smith, Michael Southgate, *Southern Daily Echo*, Testwood School and Totton Fire Brigade. The compilation team of Barbara Deacon, Cecil and Sylvia Dench, Terry Henry and Michael Southgate also wish to thank John Coney, David Effemy, Douglas Hobby, Geoff Smith and other members of the society who have given help from time to time. If we have inadvertently infringed anyone's rights in respect of photographic reproduction, the compilers hope they will be excused.

Cover photograph: Powells' forge, Eling Lane, 1930. Photograph taken by James Smith.

Testwood was once a feudal manor in the ancient parish of Eling and had several great estates. This ivy-covered fishing lodge, at the place known locally as Salmon Leap, is seen here early in the twentieth century. Originally occupied by the miller of Testwood Mill, burnt down in 1890, it later became the home of the water bailiff and part of the Great Testwood House estate. The salmon fisheries on the River Test are world-famous. The estate once belonged to the Hon. William Sturges-Bourne, who was briefly Home Secretary in 1827 during George Canning's government. His daughter, Anne Sturges-Bourne, was a local benefactress and had St Anne's church, Calmore, built in 1865. Testwood lies north of Totton and is on

Chapter 1

NORTH OF THE RAILWAY

the main route from Salisbury through Totton towards the port of Southampton. Great Testwood House was demolished in the 1930s and the cottage, the remains of the old mill next door and the Lodge at the original entrance form part of a picturesque walk around the old estate.

Testwood

Testwood Lodge and the main entrance to the former Great Testwood estate, c. 1901. The large archways evident in the modern photograph add credence to the belief that the building was originally a Calling Arch. Although largely rebuilt in Georgian times, parts of Testwood House were Elizabethan, and the coaches driving towards the house are thought to have driven under the arch and sounded their horns, which echoed loudly enough to warn those in the house that visitors were on their way. The land directly behind the Lodge has now been turned into allotments to replace those further down the lane, displaced when the car park and Civic Centre were built. Legend has it that Elizabeth I stayed at Testwood House for the fishing, fell in the water one day and was rescued by the water bailiff who leaned her against a tree to dry out, whereupon she decreed that as long as the tree stood, free cordage (firewood) would be available to the estate.

Testwood (Dower) House is seen here – not the big house in view but the smaller one to the right of Testwood Lodge. This image was probably taken in the 1930s. Confusingly, there were three major houses in the vicinity, two of which dated back to the 1600s – Great Testwood and Little Testwood, plus this, Dower House. The only one of the three remaining is near Ower and is now called Testwood House. A dower house was one occupied by a widow of rank. Once the estate descended to the next in line of inheritance, the widow went to a smaller house on the same estate. If she had no rank or means, her welfare would depend on the good will (or otherwise) of the new incumbent. Readers of Jane Austen's novels will know how distressing this could be. The Salmon Leap public house built in the late 1960s now occupies the site.

The inn had an etched window bearing the name of Ashby's Eling Brewery which is now on permanent display at Eling Tide Mill. Next door on the left was the Totton Waggon Works. The building in this 1975 image was used by the Civil Defence during the Second World War and was where gas masks were supposedly handed in when it ended. Sadly this popular pub was demolished in 1985. The Testvale surgery which replaced it was built in 1987, and itself replaced the doctors' surgery at Elingfield in the High Street. The Traveller's Rest was a popular meeting place and pick-up point for outings. You can still hear people saying they will be picked up at 'The Travellers'.

Continuing along the main road from Salisbury to Southampton, the Traveller's Rest was a Victorian public house close to the town's Civic Centre.

Still in Salisbury Road, Sarum House was situated at the junction with Water Lane. This 1950s scene unfortunately does not show the outbuildings on the left, which housed the Una Star laundry. In the garden is the prominent and well-known Monkey Puzzle tree. The house was believed to have been built in the mid-eighteenth century as Totton Farm House. As Sarum House, it later became the home of the Wiltshire family. At the side of the house hung an enormous ship's bell which, when rung, was said to have been heard all over Totton. Early in the 1910s the premises were taken over by Bert Morris, a radio and bicycle dealer, but by 1966 it had been demolished and replaced by a parade of shops dominated by a new supermarket called Key Markets, with maisonettes built above the shops. Now even Key Markets has gone and a variety of shops have taken its place.

This view from 1960 looks towards Commercial Road and was taken, it seems, from the middle of Ringwood Road by the forked junction outside the World's Stores grocery shop, now replaced by the Asda roundabout. To the left of the photograph, at the start of Salisbury Road, is a Victorian terrace of cottages called Albert Terrace after Albert, the Prince Consort, who died in 1861. The nearest house was believed to have been occupied by the Cardey family, and other occupants of the terrace included the Hayters, Duells, Lowmans and Goodalls. On the right, just out of sight, is where Bert Morris's shop was originally sited before moving to Sarum House. In the distance can be seen the chemist and the National Westminster Bank. Everything on the left of the image was demolished to make way for the new Totton Precinct, the first shops of which opened for business in 1963. The latest Totton Plan envisages a plaza nearby and some changes of route.

We have now reached the foot of Salisbury Road and the Asda roundabout and are here turning into the Ringwood Road towards the west. The Methodist church was built in 1887. This picture dates from around 1910. For about eleven years now the church has operated as a Christian call-in centre and the base for production of the church magazine *The Grapevine*. The old cottages next to the church have recently been incorporated into Creature Comforts, a shop which sells animal food and supplies. There used to be a café on the site called the Cottage Café, which was very popular, especially during the 1950s. However, it gradually declined over the years, becoming what was known as a 'bikers' café' and, after some unfortunate incidents was eventually forced to shut down.

This lovely old cottage in Pope's Lane was the house of the Avery family. At the extreme right of the picture can be seen a chimney which belonged to the thatched cottage on the corner of Water Lane. Seen here around 1930, Jack Avery and his wife are in the near doorway, with Mr and Mrs Jack Ashley and a third man in the second doorway. These cottages have now been replaced by shops at the far end of the street, built in the late 1930s, and, lower left, a terrace of houses built in the 1960s, one of which is a dentist's surgery. The base of the road at its junction with Ringwood Road was closed off several years ago to discourage rat running, that is, the popular practice of avoiding Totton's chronic traffic hold-ups by driving down side streets.

The Old Farmhouse public house, seen here during the 1950s, is sited on the Ringwood Road, formerly known as Bears' Lane. No-one knows why this part of Totton was so called, or why its junction with Calmore Road is known as Bears' Lane End. The original Old Farmhouse was an outlet for the local brewers, Ashby's Eling Brewery, and must have been quite isolated, positioned as it was on the outskirts of Totton on the main route to Ringwood and the west. The present Old Farmhouse was built in the 1930s in the mock-Tudor style popular then. Still recognisable today, apart from an extension and a change of colour, there are now barbecues and karaoke where once it was just sandwiches and the old piano. This area is much built-up now with housing estates, a post office, convenience shop, schools, a college and a sports complex. Testbourne housing estate has replaced the old Testbourne House, the railings of which are all that remain.

hot penny buns, sold in a baker's dozen, were famous in Totton. On the right of this picture, the siren stack seen over the top of the Double U library shows the position of the war-time siren sited nearby in Beaumont Road, on premises later to become Totton fire station. The cleaner service remained till the 1990s and the Midland Bank still occupies the same site, although the large wooden bus shelter outside was demolished shortly after this picture was taken. The Elephant and Castle is still much in evidence, although this old coaching inn seems ever-more dwarfed by the surrounding buildings. The entrance to Junction Road was closed and paved in the 1980s and is now a pedestrian precinct.

Moving back down Ringwood Road and along Commercial Road, we reach Hatcher's Bakery on the corner of Testwood Lane, seen here in 1951. Its

Card's fish and chip shop, 1960. Alfred Card and his wife, Elsie, opened this landmark family business, that operated from 1923-1999, when potatoes were $3\frac{1}{2}$d per pound. Fresh fish delivered by train to Totton Goods Yard from Grimsby and Hull was often brought to the shop on sack trucks. The clock on the front of the shop was Alf's idea, and was originally sponsored by the suppliers of Kingston Kippers, Grimsby. In the early 1970s Ernest Card and his wife, Hilda, gave the clock a new design in memory of Ernest's father. Third generation June and her husband Ian Aldous, refurbished the clock during the 1980s. Today the clock is an historical reminder to many of the local residents, while the shop is now one of Totton's popular Chinese takeaways. (Card family history courtesy of June Aldous)

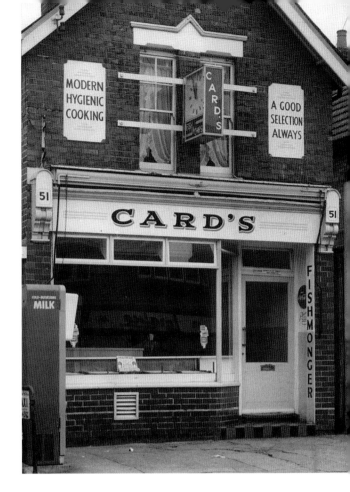

Commercial Road North in the 1950s, showing the route to nearby Southampton with the bell tower of St Teresa's church in the distance. The buildings remain virtually the same, except for the odd extension. The petrol pumps within a short distance of each other are charmingly dated, large service stations being now the order of the day in Totton with two opposite each other further up the road. Alfred Merrett ran Merrett's Groceries and Provisions. Holgates Motor Engineers next door reputedly did government work for many years. Douglas Marriot's friendly greengrocer shop at No. 59 remained till the 1950s. A Mrs King ran a hairdresser's at No. 63 and Lovell's bike shop next to the church was also known for many years. Today a hairdresser's shop remains but all other businesses have changed hands several times.

Continuing along Commercial Road and approaching the causeway towards Redbridge is the Red Lion, seen here around 1910. Some parts of this old coaching inn dated back 300 years or more, according to the report on its demolition in the 1930s, when it was rebuilt in the mock-Tudor style so fashionable then. The parish records bear testament to this, as there are frequent references to business of various sorts being undertaken at 'Ye sign of Ye Red Lion'. The old thatched cottage next door was said to have been occupied by Mr Moore of Moore's shop in Rumbridge Street. A lady still living in the area claims to remember having to collect his dinner from the cottage to take to him at his shop at Rumbridge. The replacement Red Lion's name was changed briefly to Henry's in the 1980s but had changed back by 1994. A garage and outhouses now replace the old thatched cottage site.

Old House & the Red Lion, Totton, nr. Southampton.

Moving back up Commercial Road in the 1950s is Andrews Store. This 1930s department store sold clothes, fabric, linen and baby clothes in the main part of the store, and shoes and menswear in the adjoining shop on the right-hand side. There was an interconnecting archway between the two shops and a broad stairway to the changing rooms and clothing upstairs. The Kelly's 1941 Street Directory lists a Ronald Andrews as a draper there, whereas the 1956 Directory lists a T.C. Nelmes, draper. Despite this apparent change of ownership the Andrews name was still retained for many years. A new complex of shops has now replaced the old store, whilst the top storey has been developed into an Indian restaurant since 1991, reflecting the current trend for exotic food.

The old Totton Toll House in Commercial Road, close to Junction Road. Built for the old Sarum and Eling Turnpike Trust in 1753, which formerly maintained the road between Totton and Salisbury, the tollgate was one of six in the vicinity of Totton and was three storeys high, making it one of the tallest toll houses in the area. The tower was a hairdressers at one time, but housed a television shop when this photograph was taken – possibly in the 1950s or '60s. Demolished in 1972, it was replaced by Lloyd's Bank which opened on 25 March 1987. This ultra-modern building with its designer scaffolding has a brick tower meant to emulate the old toll house.

Still north of the level crossing, this part of Junction Road is called 'Asda Ville' now by locals, since the back entrance of the mighty store replaced the three-storey block of Hamilton Terrace. Believed to have been owned by the Ransome family, the terrace was linked in name to Hamilton House, which had been situated almost opposite before being demolished in the early twenties to make way for a new terrace of houses built by Burt the builder in 1928. Hamilton Terrace was itself demolished in the 1980s to make way for the Asda store built in 1983, reputedly at a cost of seven million pounds. Hamilton Terrace was next to the Savoy cinema and was well-used to queues stretching past its doorways at the weekends. Closed in 1961, the cinema is now a block of flats with an extension on the front and called Savoy House.

This distinctive house south of the divisive railway level crossing, was situated in Winsor Road near its junction with Eling Lane. The fashions in the photograph suggest a date of around 1910, before the outlook was spoilt by having to look out at the retaining wall of the new bypass built during the 1930s. The house was owned by the Moores of Rumbridge Street, but was occupied by Miss Pinfield, a school teacher at the nearby National School. The old terrace of cottages which lined the rest of the road was demolished in the 1960s leaving the house with the balcony isolated. It was itself demolished in the 1980s to make way for a car park, and the only reminder is the large oak tree which stood to the left of the house and still overlooks the site today.

Chapter 2

SOUTH OF THE RAILWAY

This solid Victorian villa in Junction Road, opposite Treeside Avenue, was once St Elmo's College for young ladies – one of many private educational establishments in Totton – before becoming St Elmo's Nursing Home in the 1920s. This photograph is believed to be of Nurse Ings, and taken in 1915. Nurse Ings started her nursing home in the adjacent house to the right, before taking over the school next door. She managed the nursing home throughout the 1930s but appears to have retired to Treeside Avenue by the 1940s, when a Nurse Diver took over the nursing home. Many of Totton's present inhabitants owe their safe delivery to Nurse Diver. The front of the villa looks as though it has been rebuilt several times, the porch and bricked-up front window suggesting an earlier building, with the Victorian bays a later addition. The frontage has now been rebuilt to roof-pitch height and the building converted into a shop, as seen in the later photograph taken in the 1980s, before the present occupant, a model centre which sells Dinky, Tri-ang and other makes.

The automaton drinking cyder in Adams & Gulliver's wine shop window was a favourite with children on their way to Eling School. This little shop, or tavern as it says on the sign to the left of the building, was a trap for the unwary as it had two steps down into it. It had a large cellar for storage of the wines, beers and spirits, and also had an old Victorian railway carriage outside in the yard next to the old stables, which is said to have been lived in at one time. Originally founded in early Victorian times, the business lasted until the 1970s. The site is now occupied by the large, red-brick Department of Social Security building and the only reminder of 'Gulliver's', as it was more widely known, are the pollarded trees outside the building and the remains of the original brick wall which still skirts some of the site.

Universal Supply Stores on the corner of Eling Lane had taken over the whole of Manchester House by the time of this photograph, dating from the 1920s, and judging from the advertisements on the wall, sold just about everything. The woman seen here is believed to be one of the Batt sisters. During the 1950s, Manchester House was divided between Barclay's Bank and a sports shop. The bank moved to the precinct in Commercial Road in the 1980s. No-one knows why the house was named after Manchester – perhaps the Batt family came from there. The later photograph was taken on a quiet afternoon in spring 2003. This part of Totton is usually choked with congestion due to the constant closure of the railway crossing in nearby Junction Road.

Batt's Corner is a well-known part of Totton, named after the Batt family who owned several stores there. The

Batt's Corner in the 1920s. The Universal Supply Store occupied quite a large area. On the opposite side of the road, leading into High Street, was Lloyd's Bank and outside was the unofficial Labour Exchange, where men gathered by the lamp post in the hope of being picked for labouring work. The bank moved to the busier northern side of the railway in the 1980s, along with the chemists' shops and Woolworth's, leaving the Rumbridge and Eling side of Totton to become a quiet backwater. This part of Totton is due for regeneration over the next few years according to the new and ambitious Totton Plan. The old bank building has been occupied since 1988 by a dance studio, currently known as Luci's Dance Studio.

Continuing past the dance studio and along High Street facing east, we come across the old slaughterhouse belonging to the butcher's shop that used to stand opposite. Attached to this building is the small shop that was a shoe repairer at the time of this photograph in 1975. Formerly it had been a fish and chip shop, and for a short time, a dental mechanic worked there. The slaughterhouse was demolished 1980-81. The outline of the pitch of the roof can still be seen in the later photograph. After being empty at various times in recent years, the little shop, still owned by members of the Gulliver family, was leased to Loraine Brown and became Loraine's Snack Bar in January 2003. Loraine and helpers, Rose Collis and Nicky Organ, used to work at the Bakehouse Cafe opposite, now closed for redevelopment. The slaughterhouse site is presently used as parking by the small businesses using the old outhouses that were once attached to it.

High Street used to be the main thoroughfare through Totton from Southampton and on to Lyndhurst and the New Forest. Early guidebooks described it as 'pleasant and attractive'. This 1910 image looks west towards Batt's Corner and shows the corrugated hut of the recreation club and the group of shops which included the International Stores. The shop next to the hall was a baker's shop and later a greengrocer's. Between 1958 and 1970, the hall and the workshops at the rear were occupied by Forder & Broomfield, joinery manufacturers. The nameplate may still be seen above the door. During the 1960s and '70s a local firm called Babey's supplied and distributed paint from the International Store site. The only remaining shop is the newsagent on the far left. The rest of the shops have since been turned into flats for Social housing.

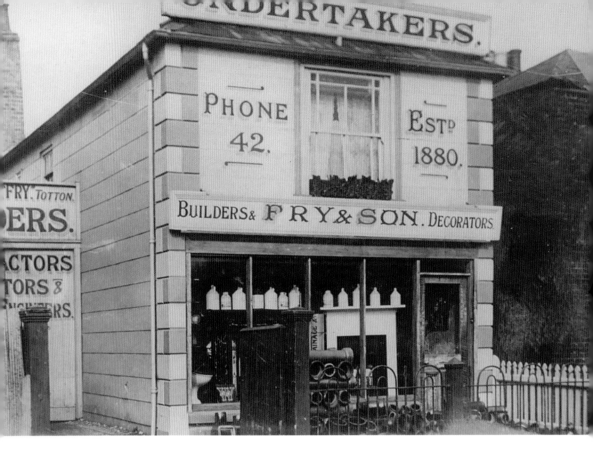

Continuing down the left-hand side of High Street, going east, and opposite the tunnel entrance under the bypass to the Tar Distilleries and Eling Wharf is Fry & Son, Undertakers,

Builders and Decorators. This image was taken around 1930. According to Kelly's Directories 1920-1926, there was also a Fry's box-making factory opposite at Cobland's House, possibly belonging to the same versatile family. High Street used to be the main entrance to Eling and Rumbridge via Station Road, which was part of the High Street before the advent of the railway in 1847. There also used to be level crossing gates, before the nearby bypass – built during the 1930s – gave direct access from High Street to the new bridges and the causeway and over the railway. In the 1960s a serious fire at a tyre dump opposite these houses meant them being hosed down to prevent serious damage. The former Fry's building is now fronted with modern Georgian-style windows.

Batt's Corner, heading west towards Rumbridge Street, May 1954. Hamer's baby wear and wool shop moved several times over the years. The Four Way library was one of several private lending libraries in Totton during the 1950s; the price for borrowing a book was three old pence. It also sold books, cards and gifts. Barclay's Bank moved to Totton Precinct, next to Woolworth's, in the 1980s. The bank and the sports shop next door both occupied the former Universal Supply Store building, along with Renier's the hairdresser's around the corner. The Hargrove's and Babey van outside and the cars in Rumbridge Street provide a treat for car enthusiasts. The modern picture shows how recognisable Batt's Corner still is today.

T. BISHOP,
FAMILY GROCER,
WINES & SPIRITS
AGENT. W&A.GILBEYS
EA DEALER & PROVISION MERCHAN

Connexions Careers Centre

Tommy Bishop's grocery shop in Rumbridge Street in around 1900-1905, when whisky was less than forty pence a bottle. This delightful shop was housed in an old Georgian building similar to Rumbridge Manor further down the road although, unlike the former, it is not Department of the Environment listed because of the shop front added in late Victorian times. An outbuilding was once a Victorian fire station. The building has cellars which were used to store wine and spirits. During recent refurbishment an old Victorian bucket was found along with wine bottles, coins and a 1940s postcard to a Miss Webb who used to lodge upstairs. In the 1940s it was a chemist shop, in the 1950s a shoe repair service. More recently it was a pottery shop, but is now the Connexions Career Centre. Operating since June 2000, Totton is the base from which staff of VT Careers Management Southern delivers services to young people and adults in the New Forest. It is a private careers guidance company, which is part of the VT Group.

This corner shop on the edge of Winsor Road and Rumbridge Street in around 1910 was George Moore's Tailored Outfitters, which also sold bedding, hardware and so much more. The late Harold Blundell of Blundell's the florists, was born in the room over the shop in 1912, according to wife Vera, who survives him. After Moore's there was a succession of butchers until the Dewhurst chain took over in the 1950s and ran the shop until it closed, c. 1980. Presently shown is a Tandoori takeaway next door to Goldsmith's newsagents and toyshop. This Victorian area of Rumbridge is due for regeneration and the shops shown boarded up at the end of the row are being demolished (March 2003), to be replaced by shops and flats – hence their inclusion in this photograph.

On leaving Rumbridge Street and crossing over the River Rum, Andrews Farm was met at the base of Spicer's Hill, and was a landmark at Rushington, prior to its demolition around 1966 for road widening. This charming photograph dated 1926 is of Mrs Andrews and her daughter, Dorothy. Passers by often used to linger to gaze at the pony kept in the front garden of the farm and the old cast-iron bath used as a water trough. Andrews also ran a dairy (now cottages) at the entrance to Brokenford Lane. During the making of the bypass, a 1600s Bellarmine jar was found alongside a clay pipe engraved with 'The Great Exhibition 1851', according to Mr Derek Whiting, who worked on the Andrew's farm site after demolition. Several other interesting finds have been made on Hounsdown Hill over the years according to *The Book of Hampshire Treasures*. In this modern photograph of Rushington roundabout, the actual site is about where the left-hand car is turning on the roundabout.

On re-entering Totton via Rumbridge Street heading east, the street is seen here in the 1920s. At the time this street was the main shopping area leading into the High Street. Many of the buildings remain, except the boarded one on the extreme left, which was replaced in the 1930s. Over the years the shops have changed hands many times housing a blacksmith's shop, a saddler, tailor's shops, shoe shops, chemists, groceries and antiques, to name but a few. The Co-op had several businesses at one time, although now it has just the supermarket. Mathew's hardware store was in business for most of the twentieth century. At one time there was also a brewery, a small church and a chapel. In the 1920s Rumbridge was still regarded as a village, though now it has been swallowed up by Totton and has become the main route into Totton from Lyndhurst and the Waterside.

Continuing up Rumbridge Street is Parsons' grocery shop, shown here at Christmas 1933. Standing in the doorway are Mr and Mrs Parsons and their two sons. Holly wreaths hang in the front of the shop, in accordance with the custom of the era; that everything should be put on display whenever and wherever possible. To the left of the shop can be seen the remains of the boarded cottage that used to stand next door. By the 1950s the shop had become a wool shop, but since the 1970s it has been a wine bar, now called The Peg and Parrot. The building has original beams inside and the Georgian windows in the early photograph suggest that it dates from at least the early nineteenth century.

Many older residents of Totton will remember when the post office in Rumbridge Street was in the mock-Tudor building, pictured prior to the First World War. It remained in this building until the 1950s, before moving down the street to its present position, to the right of The Peg and Parrot. The little girls seen on the steps of Creighton's shop are wearing white pinafores and hats, presumably their Sunday best. There is a water culvert and stepping slabs to the left of the street, yet a pavement is on the right-hand side. Kirkman's tailor shop can just be seen and the railings display the sign of Wilson the saddlers. In the distance can be seen the sweep and his cart and further on still, the field and trees of Rushington estate. Trees are still visible in the far distance today and some old places remain, including the mock-Tudor building.

"THE POST OFFICE" RUMBRIDGE St TOTTON.

Penny, the hairdresser and tobacconist, had his shop on the corner of Osborne Road and Rumbridge Street, virtually opposite where Roberta's Relics is today. He was situated there from 1926 to 1946, and this picture dates from 1928, according to a conveniently dated poster for the Sixth Annual carnival, which at that time appears to have been organised by the Totton Hospitals Committee. There is also a poster for the much-missed Grand Theatre in Southampton. A 'bone shaker' of a bike is seen resting carelessly outside the shop, possibly belonging to a customer. Meanwhile, the barber and his assistant have been called to the door to pose for this photograph. It must be early summer because the sash cord windows are half open and the men are in shirt sleeves. To the extreme right, behind the shaving pole, the Chapel of Ease may just be seen. Today Penny's shop has been replaced by a red-brick building and is currently awaiting a new leaseholder.

Chapter 3

ELING

The toll bridge at Eling is also the mill dam for Eling Tide Mill. A causeway may have been on this site during the Romano-British era; at some point between then and late Saxon times, a dam was created and the mill installed. A lease drawn up in 1418 between Winchester College – the owners of the mill from 1382 to 1975 – and a new tenant, mentions the dam had been used as a causeway 'since time immemorial'. Local people contributed to its upkeep, possibly by paying a toll. This was the main route to the Waterside area up to the twentieth century, and certainly from the sixteenth century onwards the miller collected a toll for use of the dam as a bridge, with the level of charge set by the college. The toll, unchanged for 200 years, continued to be collected even after the mill was abandoned in 1946. When New Forest District Council purchased both mill and dam in 1975, the toll was substantially increased to discourage traffic.

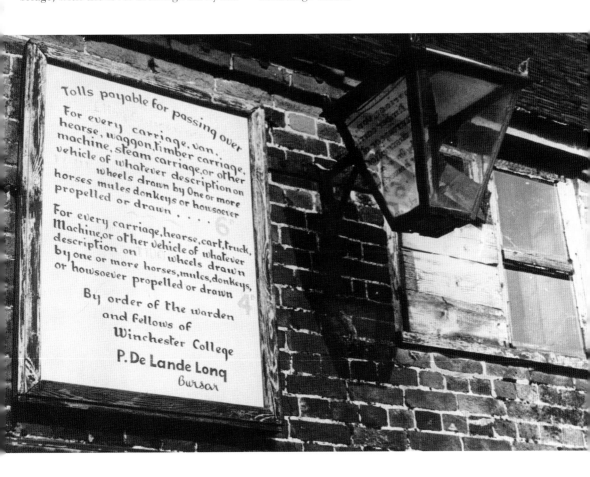

Powell's forge at the Rumbridge end of Eling Lane, in the 1930s. Frank Powell, the blacksmith, is seen wearing his leather apron and leading a pony which had perhaps just been shod. The attractive sign outside the forge indicates that Powell was a carrier and agricultural smith. The forge belonging to the Powell family had originally been sited round the corner opposite Adams & Gulliver's wine shop, but had relocated to Eling Lane in 1927. According to the 1940s Directory, Frank Henry Powell was blacksmith in Eling Lane and next door was Henry Powell, undertaker. By 1956, however, the forge was discontinued leaving only Powell the funeral director. The family business continues in Eling Lane to this day. The old forge building is still easily recognisable, but is now a popular sweet shop of the old-fashioned variety called Sweet Thoughts. Managed by Mr and Mrs Stratton for the past twenty-four years, it was formerly owned by a Mrs Mardon and known as Mardy's sweet shop.

Eling School in School Road, taken in the early 1920s. The school began as a Board School in the late nineteenth century, providing basic education for pupils until the age of twelve. The older photograph shows the girls in dresses and bonnets and the boys in short trousers and caps. Possibly it was May Day. Standing in the road would be a risk today as many of the children are collected by mothers in cars, making the road busy at home time. Traffic was no problem at the beginning of the century, however, as children walked to school, possibly summoned by the bell in the tower on the school roof, no longer in evidence. The school today is still recognisable externally; despite having survived the Blitz when a large piece of metal from a boiler casing from the Tar Works explosion nearby struck part of the school after a bombing raid. No longer divided between infants and juniors, the whole school is now devoted to infants as a First School.

Oram's Forge, Eling Lane, c. 1950. This fascinating old building at the base of Eling Lane near Eling Quay, was on the left-hand side of a little cutway at the back of Stote's Bakery, recently demolished. Children used to love watching the old smith at work there on his forge. (It is rumoured that this was the site of the original Cobbe's Forge, which made arrows for the King when he hunted in the New Forest. It is believed one of his arrows killed William Rufus in 1100). Percival Oram was listed in the 1940 Directory as a wheelwright and in 1956 as a blacksmith. By the 1970s the building had been demolished and the cutway incorporated into Burt Boulton's wood yard. During the early 1990s the huge warehouse down this cutway was being used for storing surplus grain, and at one time was even used briefly for filming an episode for a local television detective series. The former Burt Boulton's site is now general warehousing and small businesses.

The port of Eling has gradually changed over the years. The early print, posted on 14 August 1908, shows the seaward end of Eling Quay with the Anchor Inn and part of the timber yard. The timber yard of Burt Boulton and Haywood dominated the quay until quite recently. Timber boats from Scandinavia were regular visitors, though they did not tie up at the quay but further up the River Test. There was still a flourishing coastal trade of timber and farm produce based on the quay. A light railway called the tramway ran from the main line at Totton along the quayside as far as the steam mill. The building on the left of the picture is the Anchor Inn, which dates from the eighteenth century. As the modern picture shows, the quay has changed greatly. Gone are the towers and chimneys. In their place are stacks of containers reflecting the changes in freight transportation. Gone too is the tramway, though some lines are still visible.

Eling, undated. This view shows the quay from the Anchor Inn, possibly taken in the 1930s. Just a few boats were moored there then, compared with today's crowded berths occupied by the local sailing club. This very industrial scene shows cranes and steam chimneys by the site of the present car park. In the distance, piles of sand and ballast were stored on the historic part of the quay. This was where wooden naval and merchant ships were built and launched in the eighteenth and nineteenth centuries. It was from here that Henry I set sail for Normandy in around 1100. Nowadays this spot is crowded with containers. On the far horizon is the shore of Southampton, It was reputedly the view from there that inspired Isaac Watts to compose the immortal hymn *There is a Land of Pure Delight*. Not so now, though, as both sides of the water reflect industry with all the associated warehouses, containers and giant cranes.

Eling House in the 1950s, when it was owned by Burt Boultons of Eling Wharf. This was the second house to carry this name, built in the 1930s to replace an earlier building. To the right is a marine works and in the background the roof of Burt Boulton's sawmill in Eling Lane can be seen. Behind the trees is the historic Anchor Inn, mentioned in the parish records. A catamaran or two may be seen amongst the few boats nestling in the creek. These were built by local boat builder J.K. Pike, of High Street, Totton. One of the last important launchings to take place at Eling was in March 1969, when Danish singing duo Nina and Frederick had their newly purchased vessel *Algosa* launched from the quay. Today the site formerly occupied by Eling House and the marine works has been redeveloped for Social housing. The houses are attractive and have won an award for being appropriately designed to resemble fishermen's cottages.

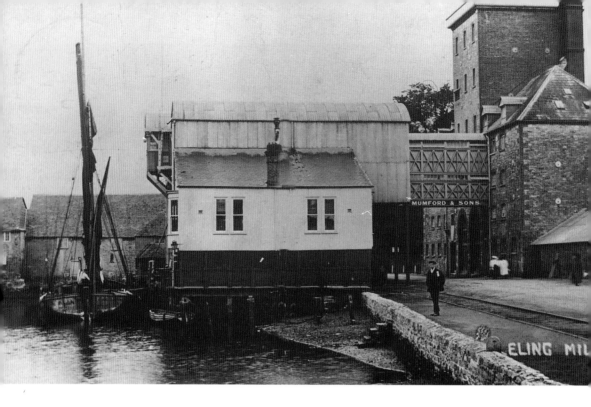

over the water on piles. A sailing barge is moored to the left of the sheds, obscuring the tide mill. The steam mill belonged to Mumford & Sons who had another mill in Mill Road, Totton. Originally a stone-built warehouse, the building was erected in the 1700s, while the brick tower was added around 1890. The building was used to assemble tractors for Allis Chalmers during the 1940s and '50s, by which time the sheds and bridge had gone. During the 1960s the building caught fire and was reduced to ground-floor level. Eventually it was bought by Totton Town Council and the base became the Totton and Eling Heritage Centre, which opened in August 1996. The rest of the building became flats for Social housing. Boats now obscure the quayside during the quiet winter months.

Eling Steam Mill, from a postcard dated June 1912, showing the steam mill to the right and the connecting bridge over the roadway to the large wooden and corrugated sheds built out

The flour milling business at Eling Tide Mill finished early in the twentieth century due to increasing use of flour made from imported Canadian grain milled by large roller mills, one of which operated alongside the tide mill. The tide mill struggled on producing animal feed, but these returns were too poor to sustain the business. The milling machinery had broken down by 1936, and the mill was completely abandoned in 1946 and left to rot. In 1975, New Forest District Council bought the derelict mill from Winchester College. The top photograph shows the state of the feed mechanism – the horse furniture – to one set of stones at this time. Over five years the building was repaired, new sea and sluice gates installed, one waterwheel and set of main gearing restored, and one set of stones and horse furniture returned to working order (lower photograph). In 1980, Eling Tide Mill reopened as a working mill and museum administered by a charitable trust: the only working tide mill in the world.

The Old Mill at Eling, c. 1910. The old cottage attached to the mill reflects its eighteenth-century origins and was the mill house. The Mackrell family lived there with a large brood of children. Both husband and wife took turns to collect tolls at the tollgate. Generations of the family were associated with the mill for over 100 years. The photograph shows some of the Mackrell family at the toll booth and in front of the gate. Several children are in their Sunday best. To the right is one of the pillars to the entrance of Downs House, which gave its name to the Downs Park estate. Next to the pillar can just be seen the roof of the lodge. The mill house was demolished in 1962 being considered too dilapidated for restoration. The recent photograph shows the new entrance building and shop that replaced the house, the pinch points that have replaced the gate, and the new toll booth for the still collected tolls.

Eling Causeway, posted April 1909. The church can be seen at the top of Eling Hill. Cottages down the side of the hill have long gone, replaced by a grassy area with benches for those needing to rest while going up the hill. This seating area is owned by the British Legion and, although unmarked, is there to commemorate the dead of two world wars. The start of the new cemetery is seen on a rise to the far right. On the side of the bridge are the workings of the sluice gates belonging to the tide mill. To the left is the Lodge to The Grove, a large eighteenth-century house, now a Listed building. This whole area is much wooded now. The church is almost hidden by the giant Holm Oak belonging to Church Gate House, the other half of The Grove, which was divided in two in the early 1950s. The Lodge has now been replaced by a new bungalow and graves have spread down the cemetery hill.

Eling Causeway. Southampton

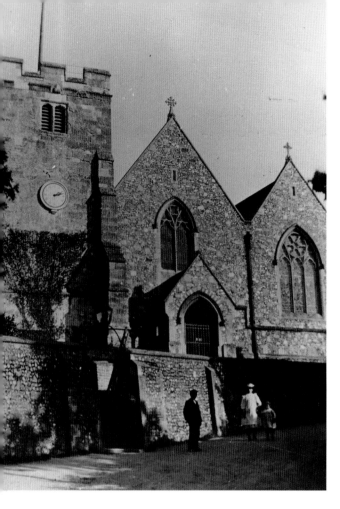

A view of Eling church from the hill, c. 1906, with a group by the lower gates, including the lamplighter. The outside of the church has changed little and the grey stone building on the hill remains a familiar landmark for locals. There was a church on the hill at the time of the Domesday survey, though it was just a small rectangular building. The side aisles were added in the Middle Ages, perhaps as the population grew before the Black Death of the mid-fourteenth century, while the tower was added in Tudor times. Considering the narrowness of the road at this point, it seems hard to believe that a group of cottages once stood in front of the church, thought to be the 'Church house' mentioned in parish records. They were demolished around 1870, when the present stone and flint wall of the churchyard was constructed. Eling church has had a few famous visitors, one being Richard Cromwell, son of the Great Protector, who officiated at a wedding in the seventeenth century. Eling Hill is not quite as peaceful in 2003 as it was a century earlier, despite the ever-increasing tolls still charged to travel across the causeway, and caution is needed when climbing the hill.

Eling church interior, around 1938/39, showing the 1500s painting of The Last Supper over the High Altar. Apart from the carved screen, added as a memorial to the dead of the First World War, the church had changed little since 1865 when it was reordered by the architect Benjamin Ferrey. Ferrey had stripped out the old mixed pews and the gallery and replaced the painting with a stone reredos of The Nativity, which dominated the High Altar. The painting, however, was returned to its original position by 1917. The later photograph shows the interior after a reordering in the early 1990s. The brass candelabra have gone and the pews in the body of the church have been replaced with beech wood chairs. The pulpit has moved to the side of the church and the chair stalls have also been replaced with chairs. However, the painting still presides over the High Altar, though most services now take place using the Nave Altar reflecting changing patterns of worship.

Eling Cottages, c. 1905. The gentleman sitting on the wall is a Mr James Stokes. Mrs Bush (née Stokes) later lived in the house next door to the seated figure. The Whites and later Harry Crook lived in the other of the three dwellings. These three cottages once formed a single dwelling, dating from the early sixteenth century and believed to have formerly been Eling Manor. The place is Grade II Listed. Many additions have taken place over the years, but the discerning passer-by may note the unevenly carved brackets of original date supporting the Victorian window casements under the front gables. The building is little changed today, except for the addition of a window in the right gabled wing, and much shrubbery outside. Recent renovations have uncovered more original beams, hidden for many years, and also revealed a blocked-in store cupboard in one of the cottages. A well was found outside the property, and a seal ring discovered in the grounds of a nearby house.

Eling Vicarage, 1949. Many older residents remember with fondness the 'good old days' when fêtes were regularly held in the grounds of the old dwelling overlooking Goatee Beach. Dating from about 1790, this was built around an earlier house. The Georgian windows face the water, while the rear of the house fronts Eling Hill. In Victorian times, the vicar had two bathing huts down by the water's edge. There was a memorial in the garden to a Newfoundland dog that had once rescued a boy from drowning. The boy grew up and later became a Vicar of Eling. Drowning was a constant hazard according to the parish records. Since the building of a new vicarage nearer the church, Rectory Court, as it is now known, has been divided into separate flats and apartments. Seen playing in the garden are Billy Taylor (aged eight),

younger brother Sam (age two-and-a-half), and their Dad, Mitchell Taylor, one of the families now sharing the former vicarage and its garden.

Christine Gigg, in the foreground. Both girls were from Junction Road, Totton. The old thatched cottage dated from the eighteenth century and was home for most of its time to members of the Crook family, several generations of whom worked as builders and carpenters locally, were represented on the church council, and were members of the church choir. Ann Taylor, who had lived nearby at the Village Bells all of her ninety-odd years, married a Crook and ran the pub for many years as Ann Crook. The last inhabitant of the cottage was said to have been a Miss Crook, a schoolteacher. The building was demolished in the 1980s and all that remains are moss-covered bricks and tangled undergrowth. The recent photograph shows Christine's niece, Sue Gannon and her daughter, Bridie, in front of the now-overgrown site in Bury Lane.

Cole's Cottage looking towards the Village Bells, April 1958, with Monica Hill and little neighbour,

A house in Rumbridge Street decorated to celebrate the Coronation in 1937 of King George VI and his Queen Consort, Elizabeth. This is one of many photographs of decorated houses taken locally at this time, showing how popular the royal couple were – no doubt in part a reaction to all the uncertainty and scandal involving the abdication of Edward VIII the previous year. At the time of the photograph, the house was occupied by the Cassell family, who were still residing there in 1956 according to the Directory. Still recognisable above the shop facade, this building was for many years Burton's dry cleaners. The building to the left used to be part of the former Ashby's Brewery, but now houses several shops and flats. Burton's closed in 2002 and is now empty and awaiting demolition as part of the regeneration of this part of Totton under the new Totton Plan.

Chapter 4

EVENTS AND CELEBRATIONS

Totton May Day celebrations, 1913. This charming picture shows a group of mainly girls, with a sprinkling of boys and a couple of adults, preparing to dance around a maypole in the grounds of Rushington House, which has since been demolished and replaced by the Rushington Park housing estate. Maypole dancing was and still is a traditional, mainly village, festival to celebrate the coming of spring and the crowning of the May queen. Coloured ribbons are held by the children who dance around the maypole weaving intricate patterns around it. Maypole dancing is still very much with us, especially at Eling, as can be seen in the photograph, taken in 2002, of the children of Eling School, dancing in front of the newly-crowned May queen, who now has a king to accompany her. Eling schoolchildren have delighted many people over the years with their dancing at local events, such as National Mills Day at the nearby Tide Mill – adding a touch of Merrie England to festivities.

May Day at the Old National School, 1915. This school at the bottom end of Rumbridge Street was replaced by the new Eling School in late Victorian times. The old school building was later used for several decades as the local 'Welfare', where children's eyes and teeth were checked. It then became a grain merchant's shop and is now a glazing business. Many photographs exist of local May Day celebrations, which appear to have been enthusiastically embraced. This photograph is especially pretty, showing the girls wearing white dresses with bonnets or garlands in their hair. The ribbon-bound maypole is in the centre of the group and it looks as if some boys have been encouraged to dress up as jesters. The man on the left is believed to be the Headmaster, Captain Haynes. The later photograph of Eling Infant School dates from 1995 and shows the children and staff dressed in Victorian clothes as part of the school's Centenary celebrations. (Photograph courtesy of Eling School)

Ashby's Ragtime Band, 1912/13. Carnival parades were very popular with residents of Totton and Eling. In this picture, employees of Ashby's Eling Brewery are dressed up for Totton's annual carnival. Situated in Rumbridge Street, the brewery supplied a number of public houses in the district and was one of Totton's leading businesses until it closed in 1921. The later image shows the diversity of amusements enjoyed locally. On this occasion members of Lord Goring's Regiment of Foot (The English Civil War Society) engaged in 'battle' during a display as part of a Glebe Fair, held on land at the rear of Eling church in the early 1980s. Society members frequently travel to distant parts of the country to stage re-enactments of seventeenth-century warfare, helping to raise money for charity. During the Civil War itself, the nearby bridge over the River Test at Redbridge was destroyed by Royalist soldiers and a number of skirmishes are believed to have taken place in the area between the Cavaliers and the Parliamentarians.

Drake's coach, 1912 on a trip to Gough's Caves at Cheddar, a popular destination for tourists on a day trip. The gentleman standing second from the front is Sam Penny. Nothing else is known about the outing which could be a works or club event, judging by the variety of hats and flat caps worn by the men. There are many photographs available of charabanc or coach trips prior to the 1950s, but nowadays such outings seem not to be regarded as photograph-worthy events. The later photograph shows a modern midi coach called into service by the Town Council, and run by Marchwood Motorways, to boost the new Totton Link bus service in May 2002. In order to help the service and revitalise the local market at the same time, shoppers at the market could get a free bus trip home, subject to certain conditions. The original Totton Link bus service was about to be axed but was saved after the council secured a grant from the Countryside Commission.

VISITING GOUGH'S CAVE CHEDDAR

ELING REGATTA. 1911.

Eling Regatta, 1911. The regatta took place in Eling Channel and on the foreshore of Goatee Beach, with land events on the Glebe fields behind the church. This popular diversion took place regularly until 1914, when it was discontinued for many years. It was revived recently by Eling Sailing Club to celebrate the Millennium, alongside an Old Time Fayre, and again in 2002 to celebrate the Queen's Golden Jubilee. In the early picture the far shore is just a haze. People can be seen in relaxed mood enjoying the event, schoolboys in stiff white collars, women wearing long dresses, skirts and large hats and men wearing straw boaters. By contrast, the recent photograph taken at the Jubilee Regatta and Fayre shows the modern trend for casual dress. The Glebe fields are now a picnic park. The container terminals of Southampton may just be seen to the left of the scene, and ubiquitous pylons overshadow the tents and other attractions.

Totton Bible class football team. An intriguing photograph for although it is dated 1912 the football in the picture is clearly marked 1913/14. It looks as though the image was taken on the Glebe fields behind the vicarage, which is feasible as it was a Bible class. There were apparently so many football teams connected with Eling church at the time, that it gave rise to the belief that attendance at Bible class was influenced more by the chance to join the football team than by interest in the Bible. Today there are not only teams for boys and young men but also for girls. Testwood School has several girls' football teams. This picture of one of them was taken in 2002 at a sponsored match. (Photograph courtesy of *Southern Daily Echo*)

Fundraising, 1927-style. This group of women outside the Chapel of Ease in Rumbridge Street are organising a Penny Trail (a line of donated pennies) in aid of Empire Day, and also encouraging more people to 'Buy British Empire Goods' –

that is, goods from the colonies. Fundraising for charitable causes has always been with us and never more so than before the welfare system came into being in the late 1940s, when times were especially hard for the low-paid. Some of the women in the photograph are named, from left to right; Mrs Andrews, Mrs Fred Burt, Mrs Elliott, Mrs Gulliver, Kathleen Johnson, Mrs Chilcott and Hilda Stokes, with Eva and Nancy Batten far right and the boy with the sou'wester, John Gulliver. The modern photograph shows fundraising at the Heritage Centre's Courtyard Sale in May 2002. This was organised by the Historical Society and included stalls run by dedicated members of the society, the RNLI, Eling St Mary's church, Colbury church and others. Fundraising, it seems, is here to stay!

Totton football team, 1924/1925. Totton Football Club is one of the oldest football clubs in the country, founded in 1885 as a result of a public meeting at the old Red Lion Hotel. The club is now the owner of the Testwood ground, bought in 1933 for £1,500 from the Great Testwood Park estate. Prior to that, the club played on various grounds in the area, including Downs Park and Mayfield Park. J. Titchener, middle of the top-back row, was the goalkeeper who afterwards signed professional forms for Southampton and later played for Peterborough. In 1973, Totton Football Club amalgamated with Totton Athletic and became AFC Totton. (Photograph and information courtesy of Peter Chilcott, first left, middle row). Today AFC Totton football team can regularly be seen playing by the floodlights that came as the result of the amalgamation. The present Totton football team is pictured on their pitch at the start of the 2002/3 season.

No. 7. TOTTON CARNIVAL 1926.

Totton carnival procession, Bartram Road, Eling, in 1926. This model racing car, towed by a donkey, hardly seems indicative of speed. The house in the background of the image was called Borrowdale. The donkey is said to have belonged to Wallers, the greengrocer in Rumbridge Street, while the cart was made by Austin Burt, brother of Charles Burt. The 'driver' is not known. The modern carnival photograph in Salisbury Road was taken in 2002 during the Queen's Jubilee year, hence the flags. The train was painted blue and was called the Land Train. The carnival now starts at Calmore Industrial Estate, where the judging takes place. It then follows the traditional route through Totton, pausing at the level crossing gates, which are invariably shut and a constant bane to those trying to get from one side of Totton to the other. Collections for charitable causes are always made en route by volunteers.

The stage at the Savoy cinema. An unknown event, possibly during the early 1950s. The Totton youth club frequently staged concerts at this time, and the long hair of those on stage and the headscarves of those in the audience suggest the 1940s or '50s. It seems to be some kind of presentation, perhaps to the organiser. The 'Britannia' theme suggests it might also have been Empire Day. The Savoy cinema was one of the few bright spots in Totton until 1961, when it closed down due to the increasing popularity of television. The recent photograph shows the Christmas 2002 production of Shakespeare's *Twelfth Night* at Testwood School. It was produced by drama teacher Dermot Murphy, who placed the play in the 1970s with disco music and modern language. Over 100 pupils were in the cast, with nine technical crew, ten stage crew, plus the support of staff, parents and friends of Testwood. It was a great success and ran for four nights to packed audiences.

These two panoramic scenes show the waiting crowds at the Totton carnival in the early to mid 1950s. The top image of the people outside the Midland Bank shows that the wooden bus shelter, seen in an earlier photograph of 1951, is gone. Mallinson's the chemists has replaced the Testwood Café of the 1940s. Card's fish and chip shop may be seen, and just visible on the right is the bay window of the Elephant and Castle. The fashions of the people in the crowd are austere and typical of the very early 1950s, with belted raincoats, short trousers for the boys, blazers and leather sandals for the girls, some dirndl skirts for the ladies and a couple of flat caps for the men. The bus stop rail outside Mallinson's, which people are leaning on, was there until the late fifties at least. Surprisingly, although these photographs have been shown to many older residents of Totton, so far no one has been able to identify any of the people in the crowd.

the main route through Totton to Lyndhurst and the New Forest. To the left is the white wall of the Elephant and Castle and to the right is Cottons the butchers. Prominently placed is Patricia's, a ladies outfitting shop, there until the late 1950s. Further back in the recess, Totton Corn Stores is also evident and next to it, Dunnings the butchers. Among the crowd a fashionable Jigger coat may be seen, short white ankle socks, handbags, cardigans and baggy trousers – all indicative of the very early 1950s. There is a fold-up pram noticeable outside the butcher's shop. Next to Dunnings is a sweet shop, and next to that a hairdresser. Before the coming of the railway, this road used to be called Biddle's Lane, and was once a turnpike road with a toll gate just around the corner in Commercial Road.

The lower panorama of the crowd waiting for the carnival shows the top entrance of Junction Road, nowadays closed to traffic, but formerly

These two modern photographs reveal the patriotic theme that dominated the 2002 Totton carnival during the Jubilee celebrations commemorating the Queen's fifty years on the throne. Union Jacks were everywhere. Beefeaters were also very popular, as were castles, kings and queens – especially pearly ones. The float carrying the two queens displays a winner's rosette and has obviously won a prize. The 2002 carnival must have been one of the most colourful events ever, with entries from a wide variety of clubs and groups. The lorries for the floats, of course, are available thanks to the many local businesses which loan them, and without whose yearly support the carnival would be but a shadow of itself. (These 2002 photographs come courtesy of the Totton carnival committee).

The Romsey Old Cadets, a Romsey band founded in 1963 and dedicated to raising money for charity, delighted the crowds with their chicken costumes, seen here at the top of Salisbury Road heading for the 2002 carnival parade's final destination at Eling recreation ground. Below is a photograph of a group of excited schoolchildren making the most of the patriotic theme with coloured flags, Union Jacks, balloons and their faces painted with the cross of Saint George, Patron Saint of England. It was a magnificent summer with tremendous excitement and interest for the Jubilee celebrations. Needless to say, the yearly carnival has always enthusiastically adopted special events whenever they arise on the calendar.

Coronation party, 1953. This was for the residents of Junction Road and Treeside Avenue and took place in Saint Mary's church hall, Junction Road. No street party here, because the road is one of the busiest in Totton. (Even after the Second World War, the Victory V party celebration was held in the hall because of the demands on the road outside). The carnival queen is seen here cutting the celebration cake, and is believed to be Bronwen Thomas, whose father ran a taxi service at Hounsdown Milk Bar. The little girl to the left is one of the Baker sisters and the lady to the right with the Coronation hat is believed to be a Mrs Bundy, whose husband ran a window-cleaning business next to the Elephant and Castle. The street party below was held for the Silver Jubilee in 1977, for the people of the Downs in Downs Park Crescent opposite the millpond. In the distance the roof of the old tide mill house can be seen.

T ransport has changed dramatically over recent centuries. Hundreds of years of horse-drawn vehicles, boats and barges, have been enhanced or replaced, first by steam engines, then by petrol and diesel-driven motors. Despite this, use of horse-drawn vehicles continued well into the 1950s. One little-known form of transport was the Church Army Mission caravan which toured the villages, presumably to promote the Bible. This particular caravan, photograph undated but probably from the early twentieth century, was said to have been a regular visitor to Totton and stood on a spare plot of land in Lexby Road, possibly by the side of Lexby Hall. It may be that it was also preaching Temperance – abstinence from drink! It is not known if

Chapter 5

TRANSPORT

the men in cloth caps outside the van were there voluntarily, or whether they had gathered out of curiosity whilst visiting the nearby hall. The little fellow in the large hat looks out of place amid all the men and one wonders whether his mother was nearby.

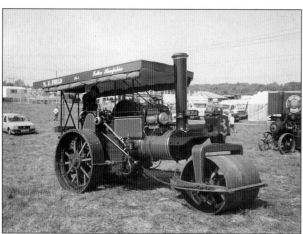

This steam engine lorry pictured in lower Rumbridge Street belonged to Peter Mumford & Sons, possibly the Mumfords who owned the steam flour mill in Mill Lane. Undated but believed to be from 1905, it shows what looks like a carnival procession, possibly for Empire Day judging by the large flags that are being carried. Local transport was pressed into service, then as now, for carrying the floats and participants of the greatly-enjoyed annual carnival. Though just what the boy with the whip is up to is anybody's guess! Steam engines still hold a great satisfaction for many and are still very much with us in Totton, where the yearly steam engine rally at Netley Marsh draws enthusiasts from far and wide, and raises much-needed funds for many local charities. The recent photograph from the 1980s shows a local steam engine belonging to N.J. Field of Totton.

John Lowe, pitchfork in hand, is pictured in his flat-bottomed donkey cart in late Victorian times. The photograph was taken at Foxhills and the family had a smallholding where Foxhills Close is now. John Lowe now lies buried in Colbury churchyard, but his particular branch of the Lowe family still has links with Foxhills. They are not, however, thought to be related to the Lowes of Rushington who lived in a thatched cottage off Rushington Lane. Few of the many farms and smallholdings that used to abound survive today, but one of those still in operation locally is Cole's Farm at Eling. Dating back to the 1800s, and leased for two generations to the Abraham family, the farm is now a dairy and beef cattle farm run by George

Abraham and wife, Pauline. Their elder son, William, is pictured driving a 1947 Fordson tractor, which has been lovingly restored to take part in ploughing matches and rallies and is still used for light work around the farm.

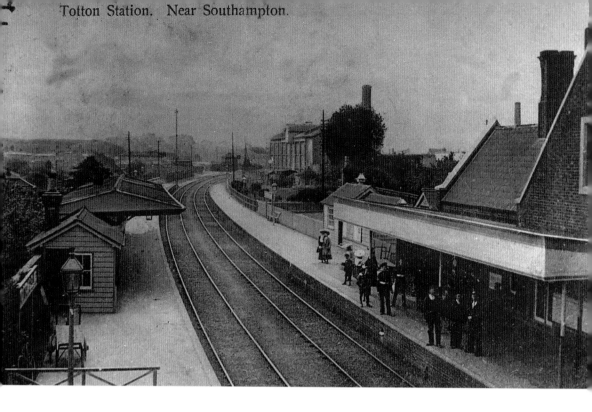

some buildings in Junction Road and on its right, Mumford's flour mill. The rest rooms on the left-hand side of the Bournemouth-bound platform were unbelievably narrow, and looking at the site today it is hard to believe they were ever there. The Victorian station building has not noticeably changed today, although the single-storey outhouse is no more, and the waiting room has lost its fireplace and dusty benches. The London to Dorchester line came through Totton in 1847, but the station did not exist until a few years later. At first, apparently, passengers had to alight in Junction Road, where there was a stepping stone to the side of the level crossing gate. Nowadays, the trains are diesel, not steam, and the doors are remote-controlled.

Totton railway station, on a postcard dated 3 June 1910. It shows the railway track heading west towards the level crossing. In the centre background the signal box can be seen, to its left

This platform scene from Totton station dates from 1910, judging by the fashions. The lady in black could be wearing 'widows weeds'. In those days some widows continued wearing black for the rest of their lives. The large hats worn by the other ladies, so typical of the Edwardian era, are now making a comeback, although only for special occasions. People do not wear hats all the time now as they once did. It may be that, as this platform was on the holiday route to the west, the ladies were travelling to Bournemouth or even further afield. The train was powered by steam, and the coal bunker can be seen to the left. The first carriage looks incredibly dusty, has sliding doors and is perhaps the goods wagon, though this is unusual as they were latterly placed at the rear of the train. The modern train is much more high-powered, sleek, fuelled by diesel and comfortable, except during the rush hour.

TOTTON STATION.

kept horse and cart was a Mr Gamage, the owner of the dairy. The young lad seen assisting him is named as Ernie Powell. In the background may just be seen what looks like a coupe car or van. Several dairies used to operate in and around Totton, some until quite recently, but Cole's Farm at Eling is the only one still operational. Farmer's wife, Pauline Abraham, is shown in the milking shed electronically milking cows, a batch of eight at a time. The milk is then piped to a refrigerated tank and kept below four degrees centigrade. Every other day it is collected by milk tanker and taken away for processing, usually to the Co-op milking depot at Portsmouth. The farm has sixty-eight Holstein Friesian cows, 120 beef cattle and farms 200 acres leased from the Barker Mill estates.

The horse-drawn milk float belonging to Hampshire Farm Dairies is pictured delivering milk by the churn during the 1930s. The driver of this well-

Eling Wharf and a large sailing vessel, *Daisy*, with a party of men aboard. In the background may be seen a square-rigged sailing vessel and a steam crane. On the opposite shore the church and Grove House are just visible through the trees. The *Daisy* is being pulled to the edge of the wharf by a boat hook, but what prompted this occasion is not evident. The boat was known to be owned by a Mr Kimber in 1920, had been used as a committee boat during the 1912 regatta, and was typical of the sort of boat that regularly called at the steam mill. Eling, nowadays, is very much taken over with yachts which are managed by Eling Sailing Club, and members look forward to sailing trips at weekends. The opposite shore is still thickly wooded and is now open to the public for a pleasant walk around to Goatee beach and the picnic area. The wharf is now used for storage of freight containers.

A reminder that traffic hold-ups are nothing new! This picture, taken in 1930, shows traffic halted on the old stone bridge spanning the River Test. This was the ancient approach to Totton and the west from Southampton, and the hold-up was caused by the need to cross the Southampton to Salisbury railway line at Redbridge. On the left, a new road bridge, opened soon afterwards, can be seen under construction. The old bridge was the one that replaced the bridge destroyed during the Civil War. Reputedly, it took some time before it could be rebuilt because neither side of the river would accept the responsibility. Nowadays the crossing gates and the signal box are gone, access from the Redbridge side is closed off for safety's sake, and the bridge's important and busy past is but a distant memory.

This horse-drawn tar boiler tarring the High Street in 1926 seems a rather messy affair. The man leading the horse looks as though he is on his second journey through the tar, while the car driver following behind cannot be too happy at squelching through it even once. One can imagine how overwhelming the smell of the boiling tar must have been. An 'old wives tale' claimed that the best cure for a blocked nose was to breathe in the smell of fresh tar from newly-laid roads. The railings on the right belong to Elingfield House, obscured by bushes in the old photograph, but partially revealed in the later one. This Grade II Listed house, eighteenth century in origin, was at one time a private school, later a doctors'

surgery, and at present is a private Care Home. Once, this road was an important route through Totton, but now it is a back street that leads to the bypass and is choked with traffic during the morning rush hour.

Burt Boulton's lorry is pictured here during the 1950s at the timber yard in Eling Lane. Here the main business was pressurising preservative into timber, mainly telegraph poles which were imported from Scandinavia by boat and landed at Eling Wharves. For a while in the 1970s, Burt Boulton's became a DIY supplier, but by the 1980s it had closed down. Totton Timber carries on the timber tradition, but as merchant rather than manufacturer, importing and supplying all types of timber as well as DIY goods. It recently provided supplies for the refurbishment of the R101/2 wartime power boats. It was formed in 1954 by the late Jack Baker in a former air-raid shelter at the Traveller's Rest. In three years it became a Limited company and moved to Glen Road. In 1981 the site was acquired for a new superstore and Totton Timber moved to its present position in Maynard Way. The lorry is pictured in the timber yard in April 2003.

This two-horse wagon, used during the production of hayricks, dates from the 1930s. It belonged to Mr Frampton of Little Testwood Farm and a Jack Frampton is holding the reins, while the other man is believed to be a relative of the Framptons called King. Traditional hayricks were replaced many years ago by balers, which leave neatly-tied bales around the field, which are then placed under cover in open-sided barns. Today, making silage is the important yearly task and farmer George Abraham hires extra help to make the winter feeds for his herds of dairy and beef cattle. At Cole's Farm, two types of silage are made, one of grass and one of home-grown maize, both of which are placed in piles, covered and left to virtually pickle in their own juices. Silage produces its own distinctive smell, as anyone living near a farm can testify, and the tyre-covered mounds are a common sight in the countryside.

Holgate's delivery van, proudly displaying its Marconi loudspeakers, outside its premises in Commercial Road at the time of the Silver Jubilee of King George V in 1935. Holgate's also operated a garage; note the strange-looking petrol pumps, where petrol was priced at one shilling and four pence. The loudspeakers on the van would have been hired out for such events as carnival parades and elections. Street bunting and advertising seems to have been much more prominent then than now, possibly because today we have so many more outlets for self-expression. Holgate's continued until about 1987, then was closed for five years, before being taken over by the family firm of Buckingham, a furnishing company which will have been open for business for eleven years in June 2003. The modern car outside the shop is sleeker and more comfortable than the old one, but the earlier models are still much sought after.

This 1930s picture of Card's fish van shows Alfred Card on the left. In 1923 he built his shop on what was then a large open space facing Commercial Road. Alfred is seen here delivering quality fish on his New Forest round with young Mr Chamberlyne, who helped out. The round included Exbury House, Cadland Manor and many other New Forest homes. The delivery service was stopped by the onset of the Second World War. Mr Chamberlyne went on to work at the Regent Picture House in Winsor Road. More recently, Ian Nelson, of Sunnyfields Organic Farm is seen in front of one of their delivery vans with son Thomas. The organic farm in Jacob's Gutter Lane was one of the first in the district, certified by the Soil Association in 1983. The farm forms part of Adam Barker Mills' estate and he initiated the conversion of the farm to organic production. The farm grows intensive horticultural crops and markets its produce through its farm shop, delivery service, box scheme and other retailers.

hands several times before being taken over by Unigate Dairies Ltd in 1983. The driver is believed to have been a Mr Bostock. To the left is the corner of Blundell's florist shop, recently extended to include the tiny shop vacated by Shergold's the boot repairer. In the centre is Moore's confectioners and grocery shop – formerly Barrett's sweet shop. To the right is Arthur Waller's grocery shop. The building, once called Prospect House, had been the residence of Frank Barrett. All these buildings were demolished in the early 1980s to make way for the link road that would feed a new superstore nearby. The modern milk float, powered by electricity, is pictured in Eling Lane in March 2003. Unigate has recently been taken over by Dairy Crest and the Testwood depot has now been moved to Shirley, Southampton.

This horse-drawn milk float parked in Junction Road during the summer of 1956, was owned by Brown & Harrison's Dairy, which operated from Oakfield Farm, Testwood. The dairy changed

These shops in Junction Road, viewed here in 1981, were well-known at one time, but have now been replaced by Maynard's Way. Maynard's was a doctor's surgery also demolished to make way for the new road linking Junction Road with Ringwood Road. To the left is Totton Timber Company. To the right the offices of St Mary's Hall may just be seen. The Woolorama knitting wool shop, formerly a grocers shop run by Johnny and Mary Chalmers, and the Wright School of Motoring, were both run jointly from the premises by the couple until the building was compulsorily purchased. Totton Surplus Stores took over from a grain and animal feed merchant about the late 1970s. Only the corner of St Mary's Hall survives from the early photograph. Visitors returning to Junction Road after many years could be forgiven for thinking they had come to the wrong place. The northern end of the road is now a dead-end.

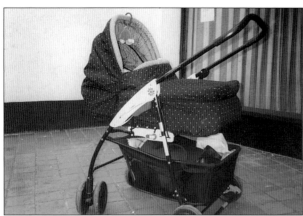

Some forms of transport, needless to say, are still powered by hand, and baby perambulators are one of them. This carriage-built pram, complete with rosy cheeked baby and pristine white lacy covers is of uncertain date. Either late Victorian or Edwardian, it is believed to be one of the Abraham family of Fishers Road. Truly an elegant piece of work, it has penny-farthing wheels, an elaborately carved base and what may be a fancy child's seat at the foot end. The handles do seem rather off-putting though, as they resemble a wheelbarrow. By contrast, modern mothers have to think more in terms of storage and convenience, especially as most women travel by car and lightweight folding buggies are essential. Although folding prams have been around a long time, recent years have seen a variety of styles. This modern buggy snapped recently in Rumbridge Street holds baby Faith Pressey, five month-old daughter of Amanda Pressey, and is typical of modern baby carriages.

Chapter 6

PEOPLE

Portraits of people, especially those in sepia or black and white, seem far more charming than the modern coloured variety, possibly because photographs today are so readily available, whereas in the past they tended to be taken only on special occasions. This striking 1920s portrait of two little girls in white with large ribbons in their hair, is an excellent example of the posed studio portrait remembered so well by those of a certain age. Little is known of these two, other than the name Landor on the back of the photograph. It came from a batch of pictures passed on to the society a few years ago with a note. Apparently they were found when an empty bungalow was being cleared in Morpeth Avenue in 1985. The

Historical Society has many photographs – portrait and otherwise – and is always happy to copy and return any that are loaned to them.

barman and barmaid at that time. The little boy with the cap was Ted Harris, who had a broken right arm in a sling, hence his doleful expression. There seems to be some joke going on in the background. They certainly form a merry group, with bonnets hanging on the bushes, one girl hugging her dolly, the other nursing her dog. The recent image shows the landlord of the King Rufus pub at Eling, Peter Spake (left), on New Year's Eve 2001 encouraging partygoer Chris Elliot to sing karaoke, a popular pastime in many pubs today. The pub, owned by one Samuel Purkess in 1852, gained its name from the King so mysteriously killed by an arrow in the New Forest in 1100, who was carted to Winchester for burial by a charcoal burner named Purkess.

This joyful picnic group, c. 1910, shows the landlady from the Station Hotel in the High Street, Mrs Harris, seated left and holding the baby. The man and woman in the centre were the

Wedding portraits have changed a little over the years. Studio shots are less common and church weddings seem more popular than ever, despite church attendance being so low. This dignified studio portrait taken in 1910 shows Phyllis Lowe, aged twenty-three at the time; her husband is not named. It is unclear which branch of the Lowe family Phyllis actually belonged to, as there were several Lowe families in Totton. The bride is wearing an Edwardian high-necked lace collar and bodice, edged with frills and tiny buttons, and a large hat typical of the time and now back in fashion. In contrast, the modern wedding of Kerry and Wayne Loon at St Matthew's church at Netley Marsh on 2 September 2000 is typical of the traditional type of wedding so fashionable now. The bride is wearing a long, full-skirted dress with train, headdress and veil while her husband is wearing tails and a cravat. Both brides, however, have chosen to carry the ever-popular wedding bouquet; regardless of fashion this does seem to be one thing that never changes. (Later photograph courtesy of society member Ellen Musselwhite and photographer, Alan Brindle)

T his classroom photograph is believed to have been taken at Eling School around 1927. Classes were mixed then as now and these children look like six or seven-year-olds. A few children are smiling, but most are straight faced, especially those boys in the front row – traditionally the place kept for those who had been inattentive. The children standing at the back and the sides of the class indicate that two classes have gathered especially for this group photograph. School interiors often used to be painted a dark red or green around the base, perhaps to ward off dirty finger marks. How many former pupils remember putting wet gloves to dry on the hot water pipes running round the base of the wall and watching the steam rise? The happier group of December 1997 shows the cast of the Nativity play in Eling Infants' School hall. The school used to consist of both infants and juniors, but is now confined only to infants. (Photograph courtesy of *Southern Daily Echo*)

Homeway Cottages, Eling Hill, 1910. This family group shows Mrs Burgess, second left, daughter Nellie, centre front and sister Edith, known as Jessie, to her left (photograph courtesy of Nellie's daughter, Margaret Hearn). This oldest of the two blocks of Homeway cottages was originally four separate cottages and Mrs Burgess lived in No. 4 at this time. A Mrs Wyatt is believed to be the woman holding the child and living in the end house, No. 1. The women in large hats are thought to be visitors. Mr Burgess was a sailor and away a great deal. Times were so hard for the family, and sometimes they had only bread and lard to eat. Mrs Burgess took in washing and mending and also, to make ends meet, undertook the 'laying out' of people who had died. However, her hard work paid off and years later she was able to buy all four cottages in the terrace, making them into two homes and moved into Nos 1 and 2. Daughter Jessie Paris had the other two. Tragically, Jessie lost her young son, Peter, in September 1940 when he was killed by an exploding shell he had unwittingly brought home with him, thinking it was safe. Nellie's elder daughter, Sally Bishop, today still lives in the same cottage at Homeway in which she was born (see later photograph).

with the beard is wearing a poppy for remembrance, and this idea dates from the First World War. Some of the names of those present are T. Over, Woodeson and Hiscock, back row, and Payne to the right, front row. Quite what such a large contingent of staff did then is not known. Perhaps the chap with the flat cap was having a day off and only came in for the photograph session? In complete contrast, today you would only find someone in the ticket office in the mornings. The rest of the time you have to make do with a large electronic machine installed outside the waiting room, grappling with which could well put off all but the most dedicated of potential passengers, which would be a pity as it only takes about eight minutes by train to Southampton.

The staff of Totton station, at the western end of the Dorchester to London platform. Thought to have been taken in around 1913, although it may well be later as the gentleman in the suit

Totton fire brigade, complete with fire-fighting appliance (1944), taken in Testwood Lane near the site of the present fire station. This western side of the lane was formerly allotments, which were moved further up the lane to accommodate the new health centre in the mid-1960s. During the Second World War the newly-constructed Testwood School was used by the fire service as a regional training school for fire-fighters – known as RT6. Canadian volunteers were also stationed there for training before being sent elsewhere. The Totton fire station in Beaumont Road was closed and moved to Testwood School and had their control room on the left-hand side of the main gate, with RT6 on the right. After the war the fire station returned to its former site in Beaumont Road until moving to its present site in Testwood Lane. The modern fire brigade photograph dates from September 1983 and has a six man crew resplendent in yellow helmets and leggings.

(Information from *The History of Totton's Firemen*, by Tom Porter)

The Travellers Rest, Totton. This was on the site of the present Testvale surgery complex. With variable dating from 1895 to 1910, this old photograph, supplied by the late Maude Brinkley, shows the landlady, believed to be her grandmother, in front of the central window surrounded by three girls holding their pet cat and dog. The girls are possibly the landlady's three daughters and very likely to have helped out in the pub as barmaids. It is interesting to note that in both of these photographs women are shown with covered legs. For centuries women were clad in long skirts for decency's sake, whereas today modern women take to trousers purely for convenience and comfort. The recent snap taken in March 2003, shows the landlady of the Village Bells at Eling, on the right, with daughter Dee, outside the main entrance. Michael and Gill Firmager, together with daughters Dee, Hannah and son Craig, have recently taken over the management of this picturesque old pub which dates back to the 1800s. Originally a beer house, it was managed by the Taylor family for most of the nineteenth century and, alongside its near neighbour the King Rufus, is a popular draw to this part of old Eling.